YOU
ALWAYS WISHED
THE ANIMALS
WOULD LEAVE

YOU
ALWAYS WISHED
THE ANIMALS
WOULD LEAVE

❀

MAYA
CATHERINE
POPA

NEW MICHIGAN PRESS
TUCSON, ARIZONA

NEW MICHIGAN PRESS
DEPT OF ENGLISH, P. O. BOX 210067
UNIVERSITY OF ARIZONA
TUCSON, AZ 85721-0067

<http://newmichiganpress.com>

Orders and queries to <nmp@thediagram.com>.

ISBN 978-1-934832-65-3. FIRST PRINTING.

Printed in the United States of America.

Design by Ander Monson.

Cover image courtesy of Lourdes Sanchez.

CONTENTS

A TECHNIQUE FOR OPERATING ON THE PAST

My great-grandfather held a brain and studied it for signs of music.
Like all the men in my family, he was a close reader and musician.

The day the KGB arrived to take him, his students misplaced
the combination to the ether closet. I see him in the armamentarium

choosing between scalpels and scopes, escaping across
the Carpathians in peasant's clothes. True, he did not love the state,

a symphony full of poorly written solos. But he could hold a brain
more steady than any in the University, interrogate its perilous

longitudes, cardinal directions for taste and melancholy, yellow tulips,
joy. I see him peeling back the hair, that quiet, necessary artifice,

to reveal a nesting doll of impulses, then reciting the cold, hard rain
of these connections at conferences in Cambridge. A halo of stage

whispers as he came as close to candor with the mind as was possible.
He understood the officer's parietal lobe where his punishment

waited to be articulated, its obstinacy illustrated in early phrenology
by the silhouette of a ram. Always the doctor's burden to reason

with that which cannot easily be reasoned. I see him make the first
incision, certain, gentle as a breaststroke in the Black Sea. He knew

how to tell the brain a story, listen when told one in return. Knew
that engine of ephemera could be a sentencing, a silence or a song.

TERRIBILITÀ

I don't want to die in a European city,
shoved off a bridge into a river,
the police never finding where I've gone.

I don't want to die in a crowded museum
home to your favorite triptych or statue,
survey the lone van anywhere I cross.

The Old Masters I studied in AP—
each century, someone intending
beauty for the others. Weak-kneed

for the boys of Caravaggio, I wasn't afraid
of what the world might do to me,
trusted desire leaves us hurt but whole.

This, my education. A kind of petition.
I trim stems on the diagonal. Burn threads.
Oil wood. From this neurotic utility

blooms a way forward. I write you
so you know I'm not dead in Brussels,
or London, or Toulouse. I used to think

beauty the point, or one of them.
Those places where even the spaces
unintended for admiration offer a reprieve.

And look, how the people are lifted
from their lives without human signature
or grace. What is this world we are making

for each other? A slaughter that cannot
be rendered or mean. Who will study it
from the back of the darkened class,

by the silence of the projector's click.

AN APPETITE FOR SILVER

My grandmother pilfered dimes and brooches,
lining them under the runner's loose corner.
To her mother, the reason was obvious.
The baker kept a magpie in the rafter.
No sooner had she slid her coins
across the counter, the bird dislodged,
brushing silken blackness past her hand.
The shock shivered down to a half-finished thing,
my grandmother shaped by first impressions.

Would you believe if I told you she became
a jeweler? That the appetite kept up her whole life,
though she was still, in those days,
a practical woman, wrapping daughters in twin furs
during earthquakes, their bodies nearly crushed
by the grand piano. The next morning,
panning for shimmer in the rubble, while her father's
reflection dulled in the gulag, mist in her starving eye.

PRIVATE CONSTELLATIONS

Every constellation begins in the mind.
Even its ascension is gentle, reasoned work.
Hard to distinguish bright from blight,
the mistreated wife, the wrongfully condemned
perched aside the hero and his hound.
A single thought takes light years to articulate,
settling on a shape like oil in water.
In this involute cartography, you get at night
what you put in daylight. A spatter of gossip
churns a minor galaxy while questions
recycled between philosophers and saints
pulsate through their destined paths
to moor at last in pensive sights. But the hands
that touched you before I had the chance
glow brightest in the galaxy tonight;
her fingers, wishbones in the shifting distance,
while below, cars bark like dogs I have
neglected, afternoon tarnishes like bronze.
Desires cross meridians to distinguish us.
The fickleness of stars shocks the native planets.

LATE UNDER OCTOBER'S SUPERMOON

A gentle inequity among the elements
for it is water moonlight wants most,

her attention, unsuited for the human scope.
In the great rivers, bodies dissolve

per their remembered shapes. We wait
in October's din, concussive music,

and it is clear why we must sometimes
change our lives, for beauty or disfigurement.

The supermoon blooms a tyranny of flowers,
white-knuckled, milky as the Pear soap

that could not save the mild Victorians.
Here, among the cradled objects,

I hear the tacit accusation in her light.
It's what we are that keeps a blight upon us.

MY GODFATHER VOTES TRUMP

At twelve, he teaches me to dress like a girl, my brother to drink
and swear in Romanian. Harmless in that way that awaits practice,

eludes danger when the light's unhurried and long. He tends
a mutiny of white hydrangeas with dexterity disguised as care.

Names failures like flowers, which culture's laziest, what color
can't learn anything at all. In his study of injuries, intrinsic

shortcomings, strangers always abandoned their own,
letting sons get fat, join gangs, rape, languishing in payouts

drawn from his paycheck. Regretfully, we looked out the window
at the world. Nothing he taught us stuck. He blamed our mother,

loved women until they became people, human in some
repellent way. It was like watching bitters made, the root grown strange,

poisoned in its own perception. Still, he suffered his conviction
he was cheated, while better days awaited, preserved in the past,

layers of ice to some murky bottom. No one knows what will hold.
The hydrangeas take on color, copper. The season turns over

with perfect indifference. And I am twelve again, November, under
duress by a language, its failure to imagine the present world or next,

a recklessness my godfather seems to have authored. A darkness that has always existed at the edges, demanding a license for the night.

ON THE FORCES OF IMPROVISATION
UNDER THE GUN LAW

The first principle of improvisation is to say *yes*
no matter the line cast by your partner.
All must agree on the reality before them.

Yes says the NRA, the Republican senator.

Improvisation is a game Samaritans play
as they run out of a movie theater,
serve as human shields for children.

Here, improvisation is also called humanity.

The principle of the gun law is that anyone
should have the right to buy what may kill
a room full of people—this failure is freedom.

I'm sorry there can't be more poetry in this.

A gun backer argues with the irreverence and zeal
of one who can never be proven wrong.

He is improvising.

He's of those men who depend
on my politeness. Says to visualize which end
of the barrel you'd like to be on.

He owns a gun farm in Florida—
they grow in swamps like water chestnuts.

Watercolorists paint them year-round,
open barrels gleaming from the marshes.

SCALA NATURAE

Aristotle organized the living world into animals and plants. That
    was the easy part.

What separates us from animals is that we think about thinking,
    I tell my students as we read the dystopias of their fathers' fathers,
though they are mostly unimpressed with unattractive people
    killing one another for the state.

        Something delicate has been lifted from them,
        a fear we could slip from our own grasp.

Always a girl raises her hand to amend: *as far as we know,*
    we are the only,

extending the privilege, though it serves so little if the conclusion
    arrived at, the thought thought through, lets the driver plough
the sidewalk in an SUV,
bans the hungry crossing borders.

        Something like a sickness of the unfamiliar,
        the way we shiver at each other's names.

Occasionally, a predator spares the weaker species
        out of something, presumably,
not thinking about thinking. And I protect these exceptions
        with amateur devotion, courage for an order
that concedes to the weak,

                        that looks and really *sees*, and pities.

KNOCKOUT MOUSE MODEL

A knockout mouse is a genetically engineered mouse in which researchers have inactivated, or "knocked out," an existing gene.

Its body and blood are teaching tools: islands of the genome's archipelago disabled, the conditioned chaos observed. Most won't grow past the embryo, designed for dissection, microscope eyes. A scientist spends his lunch hour contemplating the concealed sides of its origami heart.

How to say that suffering should yield something? How to say trespass, hope, progress stowed in the lax body, in one utterance?

Terror is imagining the human body intruded upon in this way, its furniture rearranged and forced to breed children. Someone coming in the night with helix scissors, clipping your eye color, turning off your hearing, switching out your liver for a third kidney, all of it happening slowly, like an old movie reel.

I feel my cells retreat into my fingers ready to defend their information.

In a gentler, cartoonier universe, the mice would be anthropomorphically attractive: knockouts, mice who model. They'd drink on the house wherever they went, twirling their tails flirtatiously.

Tonight, the unstudied, parasitic mice are having the night of their lives, scaring couples on stoops, freeloading meals from granite floors. Deli cats hear them pacing behind walls. The excitement of their tiny footsteps is excruciating.

An off-duty scientist is breeding something for fun, to see what happens if—what happens? Nature's mice are breaking and entering, slipping under doors with all they need to survive.

SINAIA, ROMANIA

Corridors of calves   cataract of mountains
lands pulled up by the navel   then abandoned
they say   by a dry god   on the occasion of a drink.

These, the Carpathians my father saw each morning
not seeing the film of forest from the sky.

He played the same trick for six years,
dressed the classroom skeleton in old clothes
so the teacher would tousle his hair.

Some things you never punish.
Some superstitions turn their backs to god:

>   *keep a pelt on the roof to thwart*
>   *the falling stars,*
>
>   *your mother's hair*
>   *so she won't bury you first.*

In Sinaia, my grandfather kept wild dogs
in case a man tried to steal one of his daughters.

Watered by barks, the wrong crops grew.
The hen's eggs turned a vicious red.

Some things a god will punish twice.

Now, not a single steward stays,
not even for American dollars.

That there are things we will not let money buy us
is a trick the stomach plays
staying full on water.

A god folding his couch the night he made
the Atlantic   a glass tossed
between rough stones.

LINES IN STILL WATER

Morning settled around my father and godfather,
each man his bucket in hand. All summer,
they fished or dreamed of fishing,
ate cold sandwiches on baguette, two napkins
around each wedge. These I delivered,
was given a rod. Silence was the difficulty of it.
Anything could be dragged up into the light.
And what would you say if it wasn't
what you wanted, if, from some depth,
there surfaced a photograph, overexposed
to silence and so willing to show you anything?
I grew a fear of hooks. Of course there was the eye
you most feared it entering, but there was also
the moment you cast the line behind you,
capable of catching, if you weren't careful,
your hair. The lures, some complex, easily coveted,
others improvised, wouldn't fool anything.
So exaggerated were the appetites sometimes
you had to cut the line. The men took turns
all afternoon, the luckier splitting his fingers
on scales. At night, blue potatoes, lamb
on the grill. Not about possession:
we fed the pond our patience, held still
as the possible, blind and limitless, circled us.

SECOND PASS

Months, I dream more *there* there. An evening in the old theater. A late-night drive for cigarettes. Something easily shared between strangers instead of warnings about diamond-backed snakes. Miles of corn in civilized formations. All the easily organic produce. All the equestrian Republicans. Slow circles on the Susquehanna one day, then the current racing itself.

Night brings a change in concentration. The stars are open for interpretation: kneecap or fin, dipper or spear. Often I dreamed the past in future presents, and in my dearest conjugational convictions, what was there seemed to withstand a change of tense.

But summer gives way to itself indefinitely, a stone skipped across its own plenitude. And now you are somewhere, doing something, under daylight. You are tired tonight and find rest. A great and gentle hand takes care of us. We find love, and even the failing is good. Even the itch of not finding and the absences are good, galaxies multiplying on the mind's surface.

And what might it feel like to say it plainly after so long spent finding an idiom? No one of you. No two. Ongoing. Never-love, now go. Be anywhere. Be somewhere.

THE DREAM THAT HAD YOU

wolf-voiced, not to scale with any measurable
thing, by a pail, patient in aqueous silence
as you reeled what belonged to darkness.

You drew the fish on a steel line, dangled its
enchanting suffocation. Obeyed nothing,
that conceit of fables. In midnight's knowing,

details witch to weight. How, in your hand,
charcoal became a little of the flame
that made it. I read in what's omitted omen.

Meanwhile, years pass, real as hooks. I wake
to fear I've misplaced them, confounded,
knee-deep in water. It was a dream

that had you backing off the dock
of memory towards someplace forgettable,
turning your reflection back into your name.

MEADOWLARKS AND MARKERS

In the woods of Arkansas where Monster Hog was shot, you guide a blind man up a tree. Explain the cones to me but explain them to me slowly: how a body develops between two markers, how the animals grow stranger, stronger each year.

With words, you draw a target on a blank canvas, talk of quiet places charged with wilderness. You, who hate the trigger's anthracitic smile. Who want to say *windlight* to the man and have it mean something.

Strange hallucinations, neon water in the river, cottonmouths rustling in shallow pits as couples exit the season's funny movie. Something lockjaws laughter. Something seen makes someone take a different path home.

Now get to the part where the hog walks on stage, its body fuller than the length between two cones—eight feet—and the blind man asks you if you've got one. You haven't got one, you say, just a set of meadowlarks, because a hog that size cannot be taken down.

Always, I imagine it is Milton asking, his dreams so vivid they burn through sight. Do you believe, like him, in the parable of talents, the entrusting and the multiplication? What tree bore the gun; who tends it? Not sacrifice, not pleasure. What am I asking you about terror? Your body lying the two of you to safety. Memory making more memory for me to write from. And why, when I think of you in this way do I experience that panic of misplacing an answer in one's own mind, the poignant need to find it again, between miracles and omissions, meadowlarks and markers.

HUMMINGBIRD

Knocking against my Southwest window,
I mount a feeder, inviting her vandalism.
And though a guest with too delicate a coat,
she never drops a feather, an unfulfilled parable,
while inside our losses gracelessly accrue
without logic or pattern, and we wonder at that:
what prepares a bird for so much failure
when all her body's work amounts to maintenance,
no spare change from a day's sugar water,
no breakthrough in song, no new nest.
My uncle dies on Christmas. My father
apologizes for crimes that went unnoticed
through fifty years of knowing. I've never
had a sibling, can't conceive of the collation,
but there are lessons I want to teach him
about birds, how they dare keep everything
precious in one place. The elastic safety
of the hummingbird's three eyelids
designed to protect her during flight.
She can close her lids and this spare space,
shut more light than a human eye, draw it
from a wound to guide the silence after.

AMERICAN FAITH

In Buddhism, difficult people are thought to be a gift.
This explains why I'm not a Buddhist.
I love the glib, slick farce of hardheartedness,
though I've held my human head
in my human hands so it would not
succumb to language. It was earth that taught me
names for all the planets, how to look
at an angle for the hummingbird,
dark satellite of sugar in the blossom's mouth.
I could picture that vast absence of us,
moons spinning coolly in unscripted pasts.
But when I try to imagine our president,
understanding imagination is the basis
of all faith, I suffocate on hatred's loneliness.
I can't stand the unity of my own hands,
how no part leads the writing of a word.
But this, too, is no faith that can be held,
scalds without tributary purpose. Like something
held to the light by its edges, I see the long years
ahead of me, full of voices of friends'
children's children. I want a kind of betterness.
Want it desperately. Is that faith? While the days,
impatient, fresh beasts, appeal to me—
You are here now. You must believe in something.

YOU ALWAYS WISHED THE ANIMALS WOULD LEAVE

after the 2015 Tbilisi flood

Half the zoo mislaid, the reporter calls them residents, as though they lived in a gracious, gated community. Twelve Georgian men push one perplexed hippo: no Russell Crowe as Noah, no sidekick with a checklist. How to convince a lion to return to its cage when it's seen the Narikala lit at night? The things you wished would happen in this life have you caught in old affection, fresh confusion. In your version, the animals were never hungry or afraid. They climbed the trees of Tbilisi for a better view. The wolves returned to forests in the Trialeti Mountains. The fate of birds was ambiguous as the founding legend of King Gorgasali who, hunting, shot a pheasant that fell into a spring, cooked or healed, accounts differ. So the literal king named the place "Tpili" meaning *warm*. Three brown bears lie limp in mud as police, in the ultimate video game sequence, big-game hunt the square at night. Your wish, succumbed to its alterations. At mass, the priest reminds the congregation that bells and crosses melted down by communists became the bars of cages, the ticket operator's chair. You always wished the animals would leave, their problem-solving spirits put to use, lifting fruits from markets, befriending lonely citizens. But time twists your childhood dream until it's nothing but a game of telephone, just as the bird, or was it a deer, or the king himself, fell into the waters and was spared.

ACKNOWLEDGMENTS

DIAGRAM: "American Faith" and "The Dream that Had You"

Hippocrates Anthology: "A Technique for Operating on the Past"

Kenyon Review: "Sinaia, Romania"

Magma: "Private Constellations," "Meadowlarks and Markers," "You Always Wished the Animals Would Leave"

The Moth: "Second Pass"

Narrative: "On the Forces of Improvisation Under the Gun Law"

PN Review: "Late Under October's Supermoon," "Scala Naturae," "An Appetite for Silver"

Southword: "Hummingbird"

Tin House: "My Godfather Votes Trump"

MAYA CATHERINE POPA is a writer and teacher in
NYC. She is the recipient of the Editor's Prize from
the Poetry Foundation. Her chapbook *The Bees Have
Been Canceled* (2017) was named a Poetry Book Society
Summer Choice. Popa holds degrees from NYU, Oxford
University, and Barnard College. She is a member of
the English Faculty and oversees the Christine Schutt
Visiting Writers program at the Nightingale-Bamford
school in New York City.

❁

COLOPHON

Text is set in a digital version of Jenson, designed by
Robert Slimbach in 1996, and based on the work of
punchcutter, printer, and publisher Nicolas Jenson. The
titles here are in Futura.